1
Strange Tales

Paul Groves
and Nigel Grimshaw

Drawings by Martin Pitts

Edward Arnold

© Paul Groves and Nigel Grimshaw 1985

First published 1985 by
Edward Arnold (Publishers) Ltd
41 Bedford Square, London WC1B 3DQ

Edward Arnold (Australia) Pty Ltd
80 Waverley Road, Caulfield East
Victoria 3145, Australia

British Library Cataloguing in Publication Data

Groves, Paul
  10 strange tales.
  I. Title   II. Grimshaw, Nigel
  III. Pitts, Martin
  823′.914(J)   PZ7

ISBN 0-7131-7397-1

Set in 12/14 Century Textbook by
CK Typesetters, 26 Mulgrave Road, Sutton, Surrey
Printed in Great Britain at The Pitman Press, Bath

Contents

Mrs Bosker's Cat   5

Fire Burn   15

Harry Talbot's Robot   25

Robin's Leap   37

Black Coven Island   45

Ghost Game   51

The Old Sewing-Machine   61

Jason and the Grongans   69

The Spell   79

The Voice in the Wind   89

Mrs Bosker's Cat

'What do you think you've got there?' demanded Mrs Lawson.

'It's a cat,' said Tina.

'I can see that. You're not bringing it into this house.'

'But it's lost,' Tina explained. 'It followed me, crying. So I picked it up.'

'Poor little thing,' Gail said, stroking it as it lay in Tina's arms.

'Poor little thing!' snapped their mother. 'It's as fat as butter.'

It slipped out of Tina's grasp, jumped down and stalked over to Mr Lawson to rub itself against his legs, flicking its tail and purring. Its black fur gleamed and he bent down to stroke it.

'Out!' Mrs Lawson's finger pointed to the door.

'Mum!' Steve protested. 'If it's lost —'

'I don't care,' she snapped. 'If it's lost, take it to the police station. We haven't any money to spend on cats.'

'Hang on, Linda,' Mr Lawson argued. 'Don't go over the top about it. It's only a cat.'

'Only a cat!' Mrs Lawson burst out. 'It's like everything else in this house. It's more work and more worry.'

'I'll look after it,' Tina offered.

'So will I,' said Steve. 'It's a smashing looking cat isn't it?'

5

'We'll all look after it,' Gail agreed. 'It won't be any trouble.'

'Oh, won't it?' Mrs Lawson stormed. 'And how are you going to pay for its food? Listen!' She faced them all, angrily. Her face twisted, as if her back was hurting again. 'I've got to go to work now. Someone has to work in this house. But, if it's here when I get back, there'll be trouble.'

She glared at them in the silence. Then she picked up her bag and left. No one spoke. Tina's father sat down in a chair with a gloomy face. The cat hopped up into his lap and he glanced down. He stroked it and his face brightened. Tina looked at him and at Steve and Gail. They were watching the cat.

Tina felt sad. They were a nice family, she thought, but they were all a bit sad. Her dad had been out of work for weeks though he had looked hard enough for a job. Lack of money meant that Gail could no longer go to her dancing class which was the thing she liked more than anything. Steve, their older brother, had always been quiet. Lately he had been really glum. He had spots and they looked awful. He was forever looking at himself in the mirror and feeling his face and sighing.

It was worst, though, for their mum. She was never in a good temper these days. Her back hurt her a lot of the time. She worried about money. She worried about what was going to happen if Dad couldn't get another job. She didn't like her job but she had to keep on doing it to help out with Dad's dole.

'Come on, puss.' Tina's dad stood up, letting the cat slip to the floor. 'Let's see if we can't find you a drop of milk at least. We're not that poor.'

'I'll get a saucer,' Steve said.

'There's what's left of some sardines on a plate in the fridge,' Gail suggested.

'Your mum'll go mad when she finds out.' Tina's dad hesitated. 'Oh, all right. Go on!'

The cat was still there when Mrs Lawson got home. They had kept saying that someone ought to take it down to the police station. It seemed so comfortable on their laps or strolling about the house that it made them feel comfortable, too, and no one had the heart.

Strangely, their mum did not make much of a fuss about it. They had her tea ready for her. Afterwards, she didn't say much. She dozed off in front of the television while the cat watched her, blinking its bright green eyes.

Next day, however, when it brought her a dead mouse as a present and laid it at her feet, she laid down the law. Either the cat left the house, or she did. They managed to calm her down enough to agree that Dad would put a notice in a shop window, saying that a cat had been found. She said it could stay for a couple more days or until someone claimed it.

The following evening someone came. Tina answered the door. A big man in a blue suit stood there.

'I was in the neighbourhood just by chance. First time in months,' he said. 'I understand you've found a black cat. We've lost one. My name's Jones.' Tina's heart sank.

'Yes,' she said. 'Come in, please.' Mr Jones came in, wiping his feet politely. Tina's dad came out of the kitchen.

'What is it, Tina?' he asked and then said in much surprise, 'Blow me! Mr Jones!'

'Ted!' said Mr Jones. 'Ted Lawson! Where the devil have you been hiding these last months?'

'I was working out of town,' Tina's dad told him, 'but I'm not working now. I went round to your old place only a few days ago. They told me you'd moved down South.'

'Never,' said Mr Jones. Tina's dad took him into the front room and the two men stayed in there quite a long time, talking.

The black cat didn't belong to Mr Jones and that was lucky, Tina thought. It meant that they could keep it a little while longer. Luckier still was the fact that Mr Jones was a builder. Tina's dad had worked for him before and Mr Jones had offered him work again. As he said goodbye to Mr Jones at the door, Tina's dad was smiling all over his face. The cat sat at the bottom of the stairs, watching it all with shining eyes.

It was there, too, when they told Gail that she could probably go back to her dancing. She could hardly believe the good news. The cat looked on as their dad told her, blinking and slowly flicking its tail. Tina thought it could almost have been smiling, too.

Then a miracle happened to Steve. He said so. He had a cream to put on the spots on his face. It had never worked. Every morning he looked at himself in the mirror. Every morning he seemed to have more spots. So he didn't like getting up.

That morning, after their mum had shouted for him several times, he came jumping down the stairs. They stared when he burst into the kitchen. Usually, he just dragged himself in to slump into a chair.

'They're gone!' he beamed at them all. He pushed his face close to theirs. 'Look! All of them! Gone!'

It was true. He had hardly one spot left. His skin was almost as clear as a baby's. He babbled on about it as he ate his cornflakes. He couldn't take it in at first. He'd just stared at the mirror, not daring to hope. But, in the end, he'd realised it was true. Not one single spot did he have. Well — hardly. A miracle, that's what it was, a miracle. That great old black cat must have brought him luck or something. It had been sitting there on a chair in his room all the time. It had watched him pull his clean new face about, as he gazed in the mirror, as if it knew all about it.

It didn't make their mum feel all that much kinder towards the cat, though. She was by no means as fierce towards it as she had been in the beginning but she was firm about one thing. If it wasn't claimed within the next week, they were going to have to take it down to the RSPCA.

The following Saturday morning she found herself alone with it. Mr Lawson had gone round to see Mr Jones. Gail had gone to her friend to tell her the good news that she would soon be joining her again at the dancing class. Steve was out down town and Tina had gone to the shops for some things for her mother.

Mrs Lawson sat for a moment in an armchair. She felt old and grey and tired. Her back was painful again. The cat came in, arching its back and rubbing itself against the side of the door. Then it sat on the rug, facing her, with its front legs straight and its tail curled neatly round. Its

9

eyes were like green jewels. Slowly, Mrs Lawson began to feel more cheerful. If Ted, Mr Lawson, started to make good money again with Mr Jones, she thought, she might be able to give up her job. That would be a blessing. The cat licked its fur, its head nodding.

'Well,' she told it. 'I'm not going to say this to the others until I've really made up my mind but it looks as though we've got you for good.'

The cat gazed at her as if it understood every word.

'Come on,' she told it. 'Come here. You can sit on my lap just for once. Just as a treat. Just for today.'

It came at once, flowing up to sit on her knees and then lay there as light as feathers. Mrs Lawson felt so comfortable with it that she fell asleep. Tina woke her when she came back with the shopping.

The odd thing was that the pain in Mrs Lawson's back had disappeared. It never came back either. From that moment she felt better and younger and happier than she had done for — oh — years. She kept telling the family about it that afternoon. She even admitted that it might have something to do with the cat.

The blow fell that same evening. Tina knew who it would be as soon as the front door chimes went. The lady there said that her name was Mrs Bosker. She wore a green coat and carried a basket with a lid.

There was no doubt that Sheba — because that was the cat's real name — belonged to her. It was obvious from the way it greeted Mrs Bosker and wouldn't leave her side. She had been worried about Sheba. She had had to go away suddenly, to fly to Germany in fact. The cat had been out of the house at the time. She had called and called but it hadn't heard. So, she had just had to leave and hope someone kind would look after it. She could see that it had been in good hands. She hoped it hadn't been any bother.

'Oh, no,' Mrs Lawson said. 'We've enjoyed having it. We'll be sorry to lose Sheba.'

Mr Lawson stared at her. Then he hid a smile. Steve and Gail were grinning, too. Mrs Lawson ignored them.

Tina's face was serious. She and Mrs Bosker were looking at each other. Mrs Bosker's eyes were as bright as the eyes of her cat. Her face was wrinkled and brown and very wise. Tina had been wondering about something for quite a time. Now she wondered even more.

If Sheba was a witch's cat, that was why all the good luck had come into the house. Sheba was repaying them because they had looked after her. Was it possible? Could it be? Might Mrs Bosker be a witch? No, that was silly.

Mrs Bosker smiled at her as if she knew exactly what Tina was thinking. Tina looked away. Her eyes fell on Sheba and a wave of sadness flowed over her.

It didn't matter, anyway. She hadn't been fond of Sheba because Sheba was lucky. She had loved Sheba for being beautiful and black and friendly — for being just a cat. And now they were losing her. Tina swallowed, feeling her eyes grow hot.

'I knew you'd get attached to Sheba,' she heard Mrs Bosker saying. 'I'm very, very fond of her myself. And I knew you'd hate it when someone

11

came to take her away. So I thought you might take a reward.' She opened the basket. 'This kitten is one of Sheba's kittens. Would one of you like to hold her?'

Tina was the quickest. She took the kitten and cuddled it. It was black like Sheba and old enough to have its mother's wise, green eyes.

'I mean —' Mrs Bosker went on, '— don't have it, if you don't want it or if you already have another cat. I shall quite —' but Tina interrupted her.

'Can we keep it, Mum? Can we? Please!'

'Of course you can, love.' Her mum put her hand on Tina's shoulder and Tina knew she meant what she said. 'I know you'll look after it.'

After Mrs Bosker had left, Tina took the kitten up to her bedroom. It was lovely. She had always wanted a pet. This was a dream come true. She held it out at arms length and they looked at each other. It hung there quite contentedly between her hands and yawned pinkly. Then — there seemed no doubt about it to Tina — it winked at her.

What did that mean? She cradled it close to her and stared out of the window, still wondering. Could you own a marvellous and lucky witch's cat, without being a witch yourself?

Looking at the story again

1 Who brought the cat home?

2 Why didn't Mrs Lawson want the cat in the house?

3 How long had Mr Lawson been out of a job?

4 What had happened about Gail's dancing

class?

5 Why was Steve so gloomy?

6 How was Mr Jones' visit lucky for the family?

7 What did Steve think had brought him luck with his spots?

8 What happened to Mrs Lawson's back after the cat had been sitting in her lap?

9 Who came to claim the cat in the end?

10 What sort of person did Tina think this visitor might be?

11 Why was Tina sorry to be losing the cat, Sheba?

12 What was the reward she got for looking after Sheba and what was strange about the reward?

Words

1 Write words *opposite* in meaning to each of these: 'gloomy'; 'politely'; 'shining'; 'wrinkled'. Now use each of your words in a sentence of your own.

2 Cats purr. Write the names of the animals which make these sounds: bleat; bark; neigh; roar; trumpet; squeak; hiss.

3 When the cat is first brought into the house, Mr Lawson says to Mrs Lawson, 'Don't go over the top about it.' Explain what he means.

4 The first letter of each of the following words is given, together with the clue to the word. Write out the words.

An amazing or wonderful happening (Steve uses the word about his spots): m_____

Vanished (It is what happened to Mrs Lawson's

pain): d_____

Not light-hearted; anxious or very attentive (It describes the look on Tina's face when Mrs Bosker comes): s_____

Use each word in a sentence of your own.

Writing

1 Describe three things that make you feel gloomy. They might be things like the weather, things you have to do or certain places. Then describe three things that make you feel cheerful.

2 Does Tina's kitten bring her good luck? Write about some of the things you imagine might happen to Tina, if the kitten did bring good luck.

3 Someone, it might be a young person or an older one, brings a very strange pet home. You will have to decide what the pet is. Is it a nuisance? Is it dangerous? Do the family object to it? Do they let the person keep the pet or do they make him or her get rid of it? If so, where does the person take the pet? Write the story.

4 Write your own story about a cat. It can be a witch's cat. It can be an ordinary cat. You could write the story as if you were a cat.

Fire Burn

Mr Eldred stopped the car at the top of the hill.

'What are you stopping for?' said Malcolm.

'Get out, please,' said Mr Eldred.

'Must we?' asked Katherine.

'Come on,' said their mother, 'it's a surprise.'

'How can you have a surprise on the top of a hill in the middle of the country?' asked Malcolm.

'You'll see,' said their father.

They climbed a stile and clambered to the very top of the hill under some pine trees. 'Look,' said Mr Eldred.

'It's very pretty,' said Katherine. A small village was tucked into the valley; a glinting stream ran through the middle; wooded hills ran up on either side. 'But what's the surprise?'

'It's more than pretty. I think it's paradise,' said Mrs Eldred.

'But why are we looking at it?' asked Malcolm.

Mr Eldred handed him some binoculars. 'Just look down between the church and the bridge over the river.'

Malcolm focused slowly. 'I can only see a cottage and a garden.' He was expecting something exciting, a zoo at least.

'It's not any cottage,' said Mr Eldred.

'Well, it's got a thatched roof, so have others.'

'It's our cottage,' said Mrs Eldred, unable to keep the suspense going any longer.

ALMA
TRENT
AGED 10

'Oh, Mum, we're going to live in the country!' cried Katherine.

'Yippee!' exclaimed Malcolm. He ran down the hill to the village, not bothering to get into the car.

The Eldreds lived in the town. Just recently a new motorway had opened at the back of their house. Despite a high fence the traffic noise was deafening and it had made Mrs Eldred's nerves bad. They decided to move into the country and Mr Eldred would commute into the town. The price they received for their town house was low but by using all their savings and taking out a high mortgage they had been able to buy this dream cottage. It had been empty for some months. The previous owner had died. He was a retired captain.

Mr Eldred fumbled with the key in the old oak door.

'Oh do hurry, Dad!' shouted Katherine. 'I can't wait to see inside.'

Mrs Eldred stood back admiring the roses, some of which were still blooming. Katherine shrieked as she burst in. There were two rooms and a kitchen downstairs. She hardly waited to look at them before rushing up the narrow staircase. She ran into a bedroom with low oak beams, white walls, and a tiny leaded window that nestled under the thatch. 'Bags I this!' she cried. 'This must be my room!'

'Just a minute,' said her mother, coming up the stairs. 'I've got it all worked out. It *is* your room as it happens. I thought Malcolm would like the

17

bigger room for his trains.'

'Too true,' said Malcolm coming out of it.

'Your father and I will be in the long room at the back.'

But Malcolm and Katherine did not wait to hear this. They had run out to explore the garden. It had been left to run wild. The grass was two feet high under the apple trees. They cried out with delight when they found that the river ran through the bottom of the garden.

'It's deep enough for a boat!' exclaimed Malcolm.

Mr Eldred took his wife into his arms. 'They're going to love it here,' he said.

'Thank you for not minding about the travelling, darling,' said his wife. 'I'll get better here. I know I will. Let's have a cup of tea. I'm dying for one.' They had brought a kettle, tea pot and cups. Tomorrow was the day for the removers.

A few minutes later she came back. 'There's something wrong with the electricity. The kettle's not boiling.'

'Not turned on. We'll have to leave it till tomorrow. Let's go down the pub for a drink.'

When the removers had gone, Mrs Eldred put the kettle on. After a few minutes she said, 'It's not working.'

'Well, it's turned on, I checked,' said Mr Eldred. 'I'll ring up the electricity board. Use the camping-stove till they can get here.'

But the stove would not work either. 'It must have run out of gas,' said Mr Eldred. It would mean a trip to the town for a new cylinder. He got back on to the Board. They promised to send a man out right away. Mr Eldred sat down to light his pipe. 'Would you believe it!' he exclaimed. 'These matches must be damp; they will not strike. What a start!'

'We're going to explore,' said Katherine.

'Don't be long,' said Mrs Eldred. 'You must have something to eat.'

While the children were out, the electricity man came. Everything was working perfectly: cooker, lights, heating. He was annoyed at being called out.

Mr Eldred lit a fire. He had got some new matches from the village shop.

The children came back full of news about the village.

'Now for some tea,' said their mother.

The electricity would not work!

Mrs Eldred started to cry. 'We'll get it sorted out,' said Mr Eldred. 'Go and sit by the fire.'

It had gone out!

They had sandwiches and orange juice and went to bed early.

The next day the children went off to the new school on the bus. Two electricity board men came back. They dug holes. They said there was nothing wrong and please do not bother them again.

But when the children came back from school, the electricity went off and there was no way that Mrs Eldred could get a match to light the fire.

Mr Eldred, coming in late, was greeted by a flood of tears. He comforted his wife. 'We'll sort this problem out,' he said.

Katherine suddenly said: 'Malcolm, come out

into the garden.'

'It's too dark to go playing,' said Mrs Eldred.

'No,' said Katherine, 'I have an idea. When we are outside turn on the lights and light a match.'

They both ran out under the apple trees. Light suddenly flooded from the cottage windows.

They rushed in. The lights went out!

'It happens when we are in the cottage!' shouted Katherine. 'We are connected with the electricity and with fire.'

They rushed in and out. The lights went on and off like a disco. Mr Eldred could light a match when they were outside but not when they were inside.

They all went to bed puzzled and frightened. Mrs Eldred did not sleep.

Mr Eldred decided as he lay there that it was something ghostly. But he said nothing to Mrs Eldred. He decided to seek help in the town next day.

In the morning, Katherine stayed at home to look after her mother. Malcolm, protesting, went off to school.

Later, Katherine went out so that her mother could cook some dinner. She saw an old man sitting by the bridge. He had a very white face and deep-set strange eyes. 'Hello, dearie,' he said. 'How are you getting on at Apple Tree Cottage?'

She had been told not to talk to strangers but she felt compelled to sit down by him and tell him of their strange problem.

'Ah,' he said, coughing, 'could be the fire.'

'The fire?' queried Katherine.

'Yes, before the captain lived there there was a fire one night when the parents were out at

20

bingo.' His hand tightened on his stick so that his veins stuck out. 'Killed the two children, a boy and a girl. The captain rebuilt the place. Lived there on his own after he bought it.'

Katherine rushed back to tell her mother.

'How can that possibly cause the electricity to go on and off?' she said. 'I'm going back to bed now. The house is so cold, so cold.'

Malcolm returned from school. Mr Eldred came back early from town. He had arranged for a priest to exorcise the cottage. It was the only thing anybody could suggest. It upset Mrs Eldred even more.

The priest came later. He went through his ritual with the holy water but fire still would not burn nor electricity work when the children were in the house.

Malcolm stayed off school as well the next day. He just could not keep his mind on his school work. He was worried, too, about his mother. He went with Katherine to the village shop so his mother could cook the dinner. The old man was sitting on the seat by the green.

'You've got spirits in that house,' he said. 'They believe that all fire is bad for children.' He coughed into his beard, almost choking.

'But what can we do?' asked Malcolm.

'You must think of a way to show them that fire is very useful,' he said.

'I've got an idea,' said Katherine. 'Come on.'

'What is it?' asked Malcolm as they walked back.

'We'll light a fire in the garden and cook something.'

'What good will that do?'

'We must do something.'

Without telling their mother, they took two potatoes from the kitchen and collected a pile of apple-tree twigs. It took a long time to cook the potatoes; they were charred black. But they ate them. They went back into the cottage. The lights still did not work.

In the afternoon they went back to the village again. The old man was leaning over the bridge.

'We cooked potatoes in the garden,' said Katherine. 'It did not work.'

'Go into the churchyard,' he said. 'You may get an idea.'

'The churchyard?' queried Malcolm.

'Look at the graves.' His cough was dreadful.

The children ran into the churchyard. It was not well-kept. But in the long grass they found two graves side by side:

Alma Trent, aged 10, killed tragically by fire 11 August 51

John Trent, aged 12, killed tragically by fire 11 August 51

'We must light our cooking fire here,' said Katherine.

'You can't light fires in a churchyard!'

'We must try something,' urged Katherine. 'We'll go out late, at night, when nobody's about.'

'In the dark?'

'Yes, in the dark.'

Just before midnight, the children crept out. Mrs Eldred was so exhausted that she was sleeping soundly. They had a bundle of apple-tree twigs, a billy can, water, milk and some tea bags. They had decided that the quickest thing they could make was tea.

The long grass in the churchyard was wet and it gripped at their ankles. It was cold. But it was extra cold between the graves. An owl hooted and the bushes rustled with country sounds.

They lit the fire, glancing round anxiously. The fire gave out a comforting warm glow. They boiled the water, made the tea and drank it. Gradually they got very warm.

Malcolm put his hand on the graves. 'Feel,' he said. 'The graves are warm.'

Katherine took out a piece of chalk: 'May they sleep peacefully,' she chalked on the gravestones.

They ran home and crept in. Katherine switched on the light. It flashed on, blinding them almost. 'It's worked!' she cried. 'It's worked!'

'Who's down there?' shouted their father.

'It's us!' shouted Malcolm. 'We've done it. We've beaten the curse on this cottage!'

Mrs Eldred gradually got better. Their father went to thank the old man next day. He could not find him. The village postmistress said that there was no old man of that description in the village. The only man she knew of with a very bad cough was the previous owner of the cottage. His chest never recovered after trying to rescue his children. But he was dead now.

The family worked hard on the cottage and garden. It became a happy place. Just occasionally, when she looked out of the window, Katherine thought she saw the old man standing in the garden. But when she went out, no one was there.

Looking at the story again

1 Why did the family stop at the top of the hill?
2 What did Malcolm see through the binoculars?
3 Why did the family move to the country?
4 What is the first odd thing that happens?
5 Why was the electricity man amazed?
6 When do we first find out the effect of the children in the cottage?
7 What does Katherine discover?
8 What does Mr Eldred arrange to get rid of the trouble?
9 Where do the children light their second fire? Why?
10 What is the first clue that the solution is working?
11 What was ghostly about the old man?

Words

1 Make a list of words that describe heavy traffic. Think of the noise and the smells.
2 'or' or 'er'? commut__r; explor__r; visit__r; doct__r.
3 Make a list of the words ending 'ing' in the story.

Writing

1 Write out an advert for the cottage. Do not mention anything ghostly. Just mention the good things that might make people want to buy it.
2 Describe the fire that burned and killed the two children.

24

Harry Talbot's Robot

Harry Talbot was retired. He lived all by himself
except for his cat, Norman. He led a quiet life,
even a dull life. He kept himself busy doing little
jobs.

One evening there was a knock at the door.
Harry Talbot went and answered it. On the step
was a big plastic box. Beside it was a man in
uniform.

'Brought you your robot,' the man said.

'I didn't order a robot,' Harry said. 'Have you
got the right address?'

'Course I have,' the man told him. 'Sign here
please.'

'But I don't want a robot,' Harry objected.

'Listen, mate,' the man said. 'This is the
twenty-first century. Everyone has a robot.
They've got to. It's a law.'

'I've not heard of any law,' Harry protested.

'I'll bet there's a lot you've not heard about,'
the man told him. 'Sign this. I can't hang about
here all day.'

Harry sighed and signed. The man put the piece
of paper away in a case and went off, whistling.

Harry dragged the heavy case inside. He
needed a knife and a lot of strength to get the
tough plastic off. He stood back at last, puffing a
bit, and looked at the robot.

It was like two metal boxes joined together, one

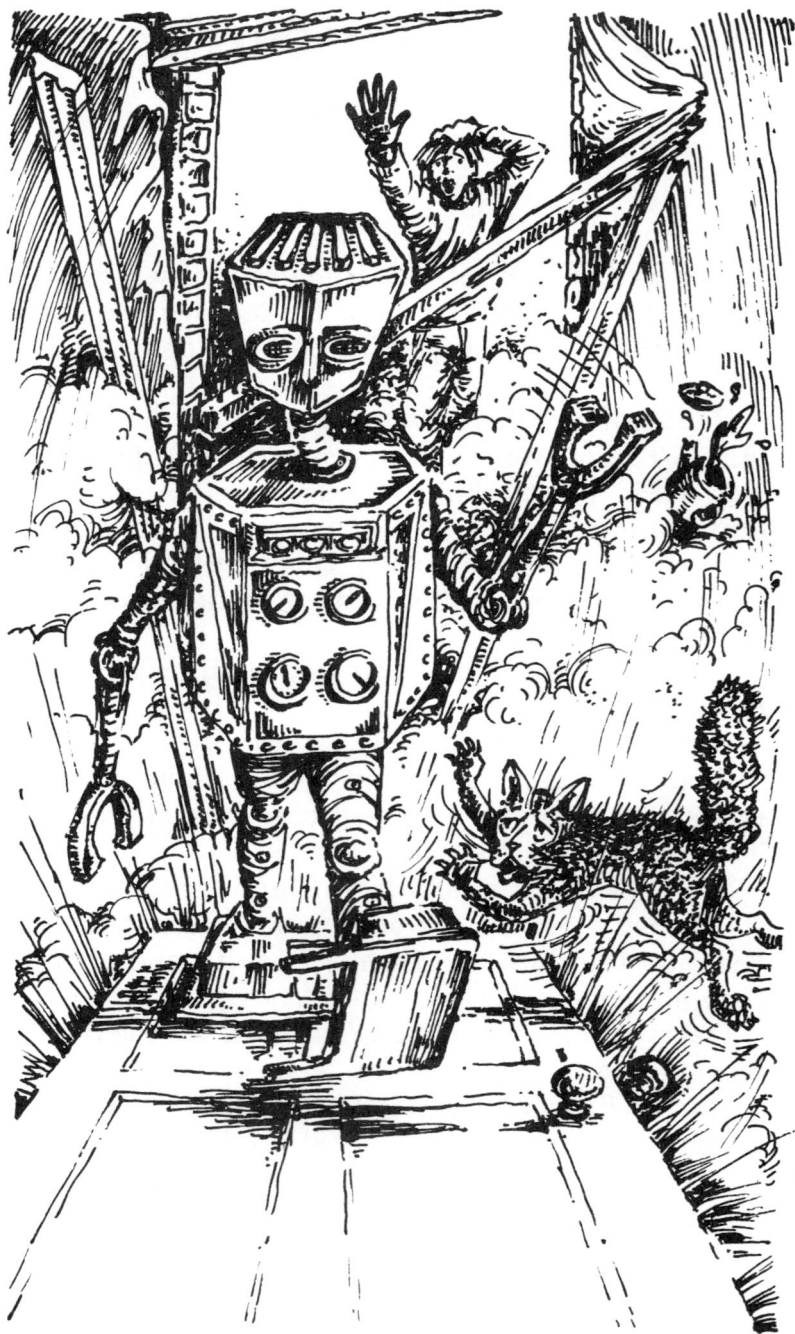

big and one little. The big metal box had metal legs and arms. The little one had two small round pieces of green plastic. They looked like eyes.

'That's its face, I suppose,' Harry muttered. 'Looks sort of stupid. I wonder how you switch it on.'

'I'm already switched on,' the robot announced. 'We are all switched on when we leave the factory.'

'I see.' Harry rubbed his chin. 'Well — what sort of robot are you? What can you do?'

'Anything,' the robot told him. 'I'm an all-purpose, bargain model.' It had a deep but tinny voice. It was the kind of voice, Harry thought, that could soon start getting on people's nerves.

'Well — er — make me a cup of tea,' he ordered.

'Tea?' asked the robot doubtfully.

'Yes. Tea,' Harry said a bit impatiently. 'Tea. Boiling water. Warm the pot. Milk and sugar. You know.'

'Tea,' repeated the robot, not moving.

'In the kitchen.' Harry waved his hand down the hall. 'When it's made, bring it to me in here.' He went into the living-room. Just as he was sitting down he heard a tremendous crash.

He ran out again. Norman, the cat, fled upstairs. The kitchen door lay flat on the kitchen floor. Its supports hung loose. There was dust in the air.

'You smashed down the door!' Harry could hardly believe it. 'Why couldn't you just open it? You fool!'

The robot stood in the kitchen covered with dust and looking dazed. It had a few splinters of wood on its head.

'The door?' it boomed. 'I mustn't be

programmed for doors, sir. I'm sorry'.

'Not programmed for doors!' Harry fumed. 'That's no excuse. You're a menace. I didn't want you in the first place. Only in my house a minute and look at that door! Wrecked! I've had enough of you. You're going back to the factory. Where's the phone?' He went to the hall table and picked up the phone.

The robot gave a sad, tinny cry. Its legs folded and it sank to the floor. It shuffled up to Harry and wrapped its thin, metal arms round one of Harry's knees.

'Please, sir, please!' it howled. 'Don't send me back. I won't break down any more doors. I'm programmed to learn. I can learn all about doors. I won't do it again, sir. If you send me back, they'll take me to bits and use me for spare parts. I've only just been built!' It began to make strange metallic noises, hooting and wailing.

'For Heaven's sake!' Harry shook his leg free and put the phone down. 'All right. All right! Stop that noise. I won't send you back.'

The robot was very upset. In the end, Harry got it calmed down by offering to show it how to make tea.

In the kitchen the robot tried hard and asked a lot of questions. Harry, too, tried hard to be patient. But, even then, all the robot could eventually manage was a very watery cup with hundreds of tea leaves floating on top.

Harry gave up. He decided he would have trouble getting to sleep, knowing the robot was in the house with him and wondering what it was getting up to. So he took it out to the garden shed and told it to stay there. When he went up to bed,

Norman, the cat, was hiding under the wardrobe.

It was about two in the morning when Harry woke up. He was quite frightened for a moment. A gleaming figure was standing by his bed. It was, of course, the robot. It asked Harry if it could stay with him for the rest of the night. It didn't like the shed. It said it was dark in there and there were a lot of funny noises. Harry tried to argue with it but it just started hooting and wailing again. Harry had to bribe it into going back to the shed by hunting out an old paraffin lamp and putting it in there.

He told Mrs Frisby all about it next morning. Mrs Frisby was his next-door neighbour. She had dropped in to see if Harry wanted any shopping done. She said she wouldn't stand for anything like that herself. She'd ring up the factory and make them come and take the robot back at once. Harry asked her to keep her voice down. At the time the robot was in the kitchen trying to wash up.

When Mrs Frisby came back with the shopping, Harry had more to tell her. The robot had broken a lot of pots. And it had lied to him. It couldn't learn. He had tried to show it how to clean the house. It had fused the vacuum cleaner. That, Harry said, had hardened his heart at last. He'd sent the robot out into the garden to do some weeding. Then he'd phoned the factory. To his dismay they had refused to take the robot back. It was only a cheap model. It wasn't really worth the money it would cost for the paper work and for them to collect it. The man he had spoken to had told him to look on the bright side. When he got the bill for the robot, it would only be a small one. Harry had slammed the phone down.

'You've been swindled,' said Mrs Frisby.

'I know,' Harry told her.

Then Mrs Frisby cheered him up. An idea had come to her as she stood by the freezer counter in the supermarket. They just had to pick a very, very, very simple job for the robot to do. That way it could be useful and keep out of mischief.

Mrs Frisby had a big garden with fruit trees and vegetables. She was greatly troubled with birds and rabbits. Birds ate the fruit and rabbits ate the vegetables. What she wanted was a scarecrow to frighten them off. The robot would be ideal. All it had to do was to go up and down the garden, day and night, waving its arms and making noises. Even Harry's robot couldn't mess up a simple little job like that.

'It won't like doing it at night,' Harry objected but Mrs Frisby pooh-poohed him. She thought it was a cracking idea and the problem was solved.

They got the robot out of Harry's garden where it had been pulling up everything including rose bushes and took it into Mrs Frisby's. They explained to it several times what they wanted it to do. Then they watched it for a while going up and down. Relieved, Harry went back home and started work on his kitchen door. He had hardly laid out his tools when Mrs Frisby was in the kitchen.

'Will you please come with me, Mr Talbot?' she said very coldly. She was tight-lipped and breathing hard.

'What's up now?' Harry asked but she had flounced out of the house. He followed.

In Mrs Frisby's garden, the robot lay in the

goldfish pond. It was not moving but it was bubbling and sparking a little.

'Don't just stand there,' Mrs Frisby ordered. 'Help me. It's heavy.'

She and Harry lifted the robot out of the pool and laid it on the grass. When they had both got their breath back, Mrs Frisby explained what had happened. She had been doing her ironing in the kitchen so that she could keep an eye on the robot. It had been patrolling the garden quite well. Then, just as she had been rushing out, horrified, screaming at it to change its course, it had tripped over the edge of the pool and fallen in. It had been too heavy for her to lift out.

'And I want it out of my garden this minute,' she snapped.

The robot had splashed a lot of water out of the pond along with several goldfish. Mrs Frisby made Harry fill the pool up again with a bucket. Then, looking daggers at the robot, she poured back the goldfish she had collected in a jam jar and left Harry to it.

Water had got into the robot's works. It could stand, swaying, but it couldn't walk. Harry had to get his wheelbarrow and let it topple itself backwards into it. Then he wheeled it back into his own garden and left it out in the sun to dry.

Things did not improve. Harry told his old friend, Edgar Best, about it two nights later. Edgar, an old Army man, was a postman.

'It's not just eager, it's interfering,' Harry grumbled. The robot was so willing to help that it got nerve-racking. Harry would start a job and the robot would stand over him, humming powerfully and asking if there were things that it could do.

'I've tried,' Harry complained. 'Once or twice I've let it help but that's been fatal. Last night I asked it to hold my tools while I started to mend the kitchen door. It broke a chisel and a saw. I'm at my wit's end with it.'

'Where is it now?' Edgar asked.

'Out in the garden sorting bits of gravel.'

'What for?'

'For nothing,' Harry said. 'It keeps it happy and out of my way.'

'Why don't you throw it away on a rubbish tip?' Edgar suggested.

'Oh, I couldn't!' Harry was shocked. 'Be like murder.'

'Take it out in the country in a car and lose it there.'

'I couldn't do that, either,' Harry said gloomily. 'It wouldn't be fair.'

'You're too soft-hearted,' Edgar scolded him. 'Fetch it in here. Let's have a look at it.'

He questioned the robot closely. There were an enormous number of things that it admitted it wasn't very good at. Edgar paused, baffled. Then he said, 'Listen! There must be something you can do properly. One thing. Think. One thing that you *can* do. All alone. By yourself.'

The robot hung its head. 'I can do a little exercise,' it mumbled.

Harry and Edgar looked at each other, puzzled. Then Edgar shrugged. 'Go on, then,' he said. 'Do it.'

The robot bent and stretched where its knees would have been if it had been human, going up and down once.

'Oh, marvellous. Very useful,' Harry said disgustedly. 'What genius programmed you to do that?'

Edgar was staring at the robot with narrowed eyes. 'Do it again,' he urged. The robot did it again. Edgar was silent, stroking his chin. Harry looked at him enquiringly.

'I've had a bit of an idea,' Edgar said.

As a postman, he explained, he was always being set upon by dogs. They would lurk behind sheds or dustbins. When Edgar came up the path with the mail, they would spring out on him with flashing fangs. He had tried carrying little bits of meat to give them. It didn't help. They gobbled up the bits of meat. Then they bit him.

The ever-present fear of them together with the fact that he was always in the chemist's, buying plasters and bandages and bottles of antiseptic, made his life very complicated.

'Well?' asked Harry, mystified.

'There's your answer.' Edgar jerked his thumb triumphantly at the robot. Harry still couldn't see it. Edgar explained.

He knew the houses that had savage dogs. He would take the robot with him on his round. At the gateways of all these houses, the robot would do a quick knees-bend. Edgar would hop on his shoulders. The robot would carry him down the garden path out of the reach of the dogs. At the door the robot would again do a quick knees-bend, knees-stretch. At the knees-bend, Edgar would be near enough to the letter box to slip the mail through. If, then, the robot was quick enough with his knees-stretch after that, Edgar would be out of reach of the dogs before they could touch

33

him.

'It could work,' said Harry, after a while, doubting it very much.

'I'll bet it works like a charm,' Edgar told him confidently.

He took the robot home with him that night. Harry saw neither of them for a week. Then he met Edgar, returning from his postal round. The robot was striding along beside him, looking important.

Edgar was highly pleased. Since being out with the robot, he had not been bitten once. In fact, he was coming to think that, even without the robot, he would be safe. It seemed to him that the dogs had clanged their teeth so often against the robot's metal legs that they were getting discouraged. But he had no intention of giving the robot up. For one thing it was company for him on his round. And it was no trouble. Walking round all day used up the robot's energy. It was glad just to stand all night in the kitchen charging itself up again. Edgar couldn't understand why Harry had made such a fuss about it. He — Edgar — found it very useful and was willing to pay Harry for it — if, that is, they could agree on a second-hand price. Harry thanked him, promised to work out the price and went home feeling thoughtful.

If it was really the law, he would have to get another robot. But that was not what was bothering him. It could not be worse than the one he had already had.

After he had finished mending the kitchen door that evening, he went into the living-room and lit his pipe. He put the matchbox on the mantelpiece, voicing his feelings at last.

'You know, Norman,' he said to the cat. 'It's a funny thing about that old robot. I know that it's silly but, now that it's not here, I miss it.'

Norman miaowed. That, in cat talk, meant, 'I don't' but, of course, it meant nothing to Harry.

Looking at the story again

1   In which century is the story supposed to happen?

2   How did Harry feel about the robot's voice when he first heard it?

3   What happened to the kitchen door when the robot first went to make tea?

4   Why did the robot not want to be sent back to the factory?

5   How do you know that the robot was afraid of being alone in the dark?

6   Why would the factory not take the robot back?

7   What did Mrs Frisby want the robot to do for her in her garden?

8   What happened to the robot as it was patrolling Mrs Frisby's garden?

9   Why did Harry give the robot the job of sorting bits of gravel?

10   What kept happening to Edgar Best when he delivered the post?

11   What little exercise could the robot do?

12   When he used the robot how did Edgar get to the doors of the houses with savage dogs?

13   How satisfied was Edgar Best with the way the robot worked for him?

14 How did Harry feel about the robot when he no longer had it?

Words

1 Choose three of these words and use each one in three separate sentences of your own: doubtfully; impatiently; powerfully; properly; triumphantly.

2 If you have 'retired' — (a) About how old will you be? (b) What has happened to your work?

3 'Harry muttered.' How many words can you write down which describe the way people speak? When you have finished, use three of them in three sentences of your own.

4 One letter is missing from each of the following words. Write each word out correctly. If you are not sure of the spelling, find each word in the story and copy it carefully: program_ed; ne_ghbour; frig_tened; vacu_m.

5 If something 'works like a charm', how well does it work?

6 Write one word opposite in meaning to each of these: sad; loose; cheap; savage. Use each of your own words in a sentence.

Writing

1 Harry uses a chisel and a saw. Make a list of other tools that might be used to repair things in a house *or* make a list of the things to do cleaning jobs in a house.

2 You have a robot. It is not like Mr Talbot's robot. It can do anything you want it to. Describe what happens as it works for you during the day.

Robin's Leap

Marian had taken up jogging. She wanted to get fit for the school sports which were in a month's time. Her mother would not let her jog on her own so her father had agreed to run with her. 'Get this stomach down,' he had said.

They went out each evening and gradually increased the distance. After three weeks they were running five miles each night. She was beginning to feel really fit. Her father was pleased as well; he had trimmed a few centimetres from his stomach.

A week before the sports he said: 'How do you fancy a ten-mile run?'

'Now don't overdo it, John,' said her mother. 'I don't want you crocked up in bed.'

But her father had really caught the jogging bug and was determined.

'Oh, yes, Dad,' exclaimed Marian. 'That would be a record for me.'

'You shouldn't encourage your father in such foolishness,' said her mother.

'You'll have to come with us, Mum,' said Marian.

After school that afternoon they set off on a course which took them through Tumble Hill woods, a large stretch of woodland that covered several hillsides. As they entered the woods, it began to spit with rain. But they did not mind

that because it was fun running in the rain. It was a hot day, rather close and muggy.

They ran up a hillside and down into a valley. Running on the soft moss and between avenues of pine trees gave Marian the sensation of running extra fast. At the bottom of the valley was a small river and a bridge over it.

'Race you over Robin's Leap,' puffed her father. He sprinted off. But she beat him by a metre.

'Why is it called Robin's Leap, Dad?' she gasped as they clambered up the other side.

'They say Prince John on horseback was pursuing Robin Hood who was on foot. He had nearly caught him and Robin was trapped by this river because there was no bridge in those days. To the Prince's surprise he leapt over it and escaped.'

'Do you think it is true?' asked Marian.

'Perhaps. If you believe in Robin Hood. The river wouldn't have been so wide in those days. But you would need to be an Olympic athlete to leap it today.'

They ran deeper into the woods. Suddenly there was a flash followed by a rumble of thunder. The rain began to teem down. Marian had never seen such rain. It was like running into a waterfall.

'No good trying to shelter under a tree,' spluttered her father. 'Not in a thunderstorm. We'll be best in the middle of the path. Keep going. It'll stop in a minute.'

But it did not. It continued to splash down, a cloudburst.

Suddenly there was a tremendous flash. She was thrown sideways into blackberry bushes; her whole body tingled; her eyes seemed out of focus.

She realized that she had been struck by lightning.

She lay there gazing up into the rain for what seemed like hours. Then a slow realization came to her that her father was not bending over her as he should be. Where was he?

She slowly pushed herself up into a sitting position. There were burn marks on her shorts and tee shirt and her legs were scratched and bleeding. She could feel or see no bodily burns. Still sitting she gazed round for her father.

He had fallen under a tree. He was not moving. She scrambled up and went to him. She felt his heart; it was still beating and she could see that he was breathing. But his face and chest were badly burned. Marian knew that she must get help quickly.

She set off at a fast jog back down the track. The rain still continued to teem down and there were still flashes of lightning and great cracks of thunder. Would she be struck again? She reached the top of the brow leading down to Robin's Leap. She half ran and half slid down in the mud to the bridge.

It was not there. Instead a torrent of water caused by a flash flood roared down the gully. The bridge had been washed away. She stopped and stared. She must get across. She knew of no other way.

Then she thought about Robin Hood. If he could leap it perhaps she could. But the stream could not have been so wide or fierce in his day. If she jumped and did not reach the other bank she would be washed away and drowned.

But the need to save her father was strong. She

clambered back up the hillside, climbing one metre and falling back a half. At the top she crouched in a sprinting start. She leapt off. Her feet hardly seemed to touch the ground and she half ran and slid back down.

She was nearing the edge of the bank. Would she get a good grip to take off or would she just slide into the water? There was no time to think about that now. She trod on a branch and took off in a great flying leap.

Time had seemed long as she lay after being struck by the lightning. Now it seemed longer as she seemed to hang in the air. She had a sensation of either being supported by the hips or being on the end of a long pole. Below her raged the white foam. Then her feet juddered into the far bank. She desperately grasped a tree branch and hauled herself up the far bank. She had done it! She had repeated Robin's famous leap!

As she scrambled out of the woods she was lucky enough to see a police car. She told them about her father and the bridge. They decided to radio for a helicopter.

She was taken to an airfield. The helicopter quickly took off. It was the first time she had flown in one. It flew low over the woods following the path she had run. She had a good view of the flooded river. The pilot and ambulance man and the doctor were amazed that she had jumped it.

They landed in a clearing and soon found her father who was still unconscious. But within half an hour they had him in hospital. 'Just in time,' the doctor said.

Marian had to stay in overnight as well.

As she lay in the strange bed she wondered

about the whole episode. She had read about people being given super strength in times of danger. A woman had once lifted a car off her two-year-old son. But there seemed more to it than that. She had definitely felt 'lifted'. And then there was that sensation of being on the end of a pole. Had Robin Hood vaulted across the river on his quarterstaff? Had she, not knowing, picked up a branch of wood? Had Robin Hood helped another Marian? No, that was too silly.

Her father made a good recovery though he needed some operations. At the school sports she won the long jump, but she only jumped a third of the distance of Robin's Leap.

Looking at the story again

1 Why does Marian's mum think that it is a good idea for her father to jog with her?

2 Where does the ten-mile run take them?

3 What are the first signs of a storm?

4 How did Marian feel when running through an avenue of trees?

5 Why was it called Robin's Leap?

6 Who was struck by lightning?

7 What injuries did her father have?

8 How do we know that the approach run to the big jump is difficult?

9 What is your explanation for Marian's big jump?

10 How do we know at the end of the story that Marian's jump that day was something special?

Words

1 Make a list of words meaning 'running'. Think of both animals and men and women.

2 Make a list of words from this story connected with water. Then use each of them in sentences of your own.

3 Use each of these words in two separate sentences to show two meanings: spit, close, minute, beating, crack, branch, lift.

4 'overnight' — make a list of 'over' words.

5 Use each of these words in a sentence of your own. Check the spellings: definitely, beginning, stomach, lightning.

Writing

1 Describe the biggest jump you have ever done. Write about the jump you would like to do.

2 Plan a fortnight's jogging in your area to get fit. Plan the routes and distance.

3 Write an unrhymed poem called 'Running in the Rain' or 'Running through Mud'.

4 Describe a heavy thunderstorm. Write six sentences or more.

5 Write as a play what Marian says to her mother when she comes to visit her in hospital. What might be said about Marian's father?

Black Coven Island

The children ran happily down the lane. 'Come back!' called Oggy. He had found a hedgehog. They clustered happily round. 'I'm going to put him back in the hedge,' declared Oggy. 'He could get run over.'

'You'll get fleas!' shrieked Fiona.

'Poor thing, it could do with some water,' said Oggy.

'There's a stream down there,' said Andy.

They took the hedgehog, which was now in a ball, to the stream. 'Does it prick?' asked Jennie.

'No, it's lovely,' said Oggy. He cradled it.

At the stream the hedgehog drank and then trundled away into some nettles.

The children all came from a children's camp where they had been sent by their parents for the summer holiday. They had been allowed out to explore, providing they did not go a mile or more away. This was their first day out.

'Let's follow the stream; it could be exciting!' shouted Teresa.

They splashed down through it, the girls shrieking as the boys kicked up water. They had to scramble over small boulders and climb over bigger branches. 'Just like the jungle,' declared Fiona. 'What a super day it is! This is going to be a great camp.'

Andy was in the front. Suddenly he shouted: 'A

river! A river!'

The rest rushed to join him. A wide river snaked its way through a large meadow.

'An island! An island!' shouted Jennie. In the middle of the river was a small island. 'If only we could go there.'

They clambered through the reeds and stood looking across the fast flowing river at a bushy island.

'A boat!' yelled Oggy. He had found a brown rowing-boat half concealed in the reeds. 'We could row to the island and play pirates.'

'Would anybody mind, if we sailed in it?' asked Fiona.

'I don't think they would.' A man had come up behind them. He was carrying a shotgun. 'Where are you from?'

'The camp,' Andy told him.

'Oh the camp. That's started has it? I hope you shut gates.'

'Oh yes, we shut gates,' said Teresa.

'Then you can go in my boat. If you hear a shot don't worry, I'm only after a few rabbits. I don't like doing it, but they have to be kept down.'

'Is the island yours?' asked Andy.

'I bought it at auction only yesterday. I've been after it for years for the fishing but the old lady who owned it wouldn't sell. I haven't been on it myself yet but you can go, if you want. Be careful, though, it's called Black Coven Island. They say that the old lady who has just died was a witch.'

'Witches!' exclaimed Teresa.

'Yes, and warlocks too, I believe, so watch out.' He grinned.

46

'Forward to Black Coven Island,' said Andy.

After some difficulty the children pulled the boat out of the mud and launched it. They all got in except Teresa. 'I'm not going,' she declared.

'Scared of a few old witches.'

'No.'

'Spoilsport,' said Oggy.

'I have a feeling about it.'

'Well, you look after the boat then,' said Andy. 'You needn't get out.'

'No.'

'Go on.'

'Oh, all right then. But I'm not landing on it.'

Teresa hung on to a willow branch as the children clambered on to Black Coven Island. 'I can reach the parts of islands other men cannot reach,' laughed Oggy.

'Look, stones,' cried Andy. 'A ring of stones!'

'Witches' stones!' cried Fiona. 'You can jump from one to another.'

All the children jumped round the stones. Suddenly Oggy shot off. 'A rabbit!' he shouted. He dived into a bush and came out with a struggling young rabbit. 'Just the thing we need for the sacrifice.' He jumped into the ring and held it down on the centre stone.

Fiona held up her arms. 'The sacrifice,' she intoned.

'Take out its eyes,' said Andy.

'Skin it alive,' murmured Jennie.

Oggy took out his knife and held it at arms' length. 'Let the sacrifice begin,' he said in a high voice.

Teresa watched them from the boat with

horror. 'Come off the island!' she yelled. 'It's enchanting you! Oh, please come off!'

Oggy turned to her. His eyes were bloodshot and staring. 'Let's get her as well!' he screamed. 'Slit her throat. Drink her blood!'

They made a rush at her. Teresa rowed fast for the bank. They clambered on to a a willow-tree branch and threw mud. Then they went back to the rabbit when they saw she had got away.

Teresa found the man in a cornfield. 'Quick,' she said, tugging at his coat, 'my friends. The island is bewitching them!'

'Bewitching them?'

'They're going to sacrifice a rabbit!'

'They're just playing,' he said. But there was something so urgent in her face that he went with her to the bank of the river. He watched the children for a few seconds then he quickly rowed over with Teresa.

The man landed on the island. Teresa held the boat steady with the willow branch. The children did not see him at first, they were so keen on the sacrifice.

'What's all this?' he asked.

Oggy looked up and saw his gun. 'Come and help us,' he intoned. 'We can have more sacrifices. Come into the ring of stones.'

The man decided to humour him. He walked round the ring of stones with Oggy, pretending to take part in the sacrifice. But as he reached the last stone his mouth began to twitch. He raised his gun on his shoulder and said, 'I have a better game. We can play pirates. It will be a better sacrifice. You can walk the plank. Get on to that willow branch.' His eyes were staring and wild with ancient magic.

The children got up slowly. The shock of the pointing gun half brought them out of their trance. Teresa watched this turn of events with horror. She trembled too much to row away.

Oggy was by now on the end of the branch. The swift-flowing current beneath him. The man was on the other end poking him with the gun. 'Walk!'

Suddenly Teresa stood up in the boat. She launched herself in a rugby tackle. The boat shot out into the stream of fast flowing water. But she caught the man round the ankles and he fell backwards into the water. She picked herself out of the mud. 'We've got to swim it!' she yelled. She set off. The others dived in.

Terror made her swim so fast that she caught up with the boat. She helped the others in. Oggy was on the point of drowning.

Andy rowed fast for the bank. As they hit the reeds they scrambled out and ran, except Teresa who had no more energy and fainted.

She came round to find the man bending over her. She screamed. But the wild look had gone from his eyes. 'It's all right,' he said. 'It's all right. What happened to me?'

Teresa told the story between great sobs.

'It is like a dream,' said the man. 'I can remember it through a mist. How could I act like I did?'

'I had a feeling about it the moment I saw it,' said Teresa.

'Thank goodness you did. No one must ever go there again. Come on, we must get into some dry clothes.'

Looking at the story again

1 Who carries the hedgehog? What might he catch from it?
2 How far could they explore from the summer camp?
3 What does Andy discover?
4 What does Oggy discover?
5 How long has the man owned the island?
6 How do we know he has not set foot on it yet?
7 Who does not want to go on the island? Why?
8 How soon are the children bewitched?
9 What does Teresa do as the children become bewitched?
10 What happens to the man when he steps on the stones?
11 What does he do to the children?
12 How does Teresa save them?

Words

1 'shrieking' — what other words mean this?
2 What does 'A wide river *snaked* its way through a large meadow' mean?
3 What is the opposite of: lovely, exciting, super, shut, exhausted? You can use more than one word if you like.

Writing

1 Write down three things a witch might chant.
2 In about four sentences or more, describe young children playing in water.
3 Write a short story, explaining the meaning of the ring of stones. How might they have been used?

Ghost Game

Robb thought at first that it was the best game that he had ever had. The screen had a pattern of double lines on it. These were the corridors of the haunted house. You — the round dot — could move up and down these as you moved the lever. If you were very good at the game, you could escape. The ghosts were weird, fuzzy dots. They slithered up and down the corridors, too. If one of them touched you, you became a ghost. Then the voice of the computer said, 'Game over!' You were dead.

It didn't really say words: it made three sounds. These were rather eerie, all on one note, as if some metal voice were trying to speak. Robb, though, knew what it meant. He found the metal voice a bit creepy at first because he lost all his games very quickly. When he got better at playing the game, he got used to the sound.

You could escape a ghost, if you used a ghost stopper. These were little crosses. With the lever you could send one of these down a corridor towards a ghost. Then the ghost would stop coming towards you and slide off down another corridor. But there were always so many ghosts and not enough ghost stoppers.

If you got past all the ghosts and reached the door of the haunted house, the computer made a different noise. It was musical, like a bell.

The young man in the shop where they sold the game had played so well that he had made it look easy. Robb, himself, had never got past all the ghosts. He had not had a chance to hear that pleasant, gong-like sound which meant that he had reached the door and was free. But you got better, the more you played the game. In the beginning, the ghosts had got Robb very quickly. Soon, though, he was making the games last much longer before he was caught. He hoped, in the end, to become so good at the game that he would nearly always escape.

So he played it a lot. He stopped watching television. He took the game up to his bedroom and played it there so as not to be disturbed. He would lose all sense of time. Quite often his mother would come up to tell him that it was time for bed. Lost in the game, he would stare at her, wondering where the hours had gone.

She was the one who wanted to know whether he couldn't find other things to do. His dad, though, defended him. He said that the game was 'educational'. His dad worked in computers.

Besides, there was nothing more interesting to do for Robin. He had been quite good at school work. Now, he couldn't be bothered any more. Miss Haston, the class teacher, had asked him one day if he was getting enough sleep. But he wasn't tired. It was just that, as he sat in class, he thought all the time about the evening when he could play the game again.

Then things changed. Always, each time he lost, his heart sank a little. At the beginning, though, he started each new game quite eagerly, hoping that that time he was going to win. Then, as he lost over and over again, the game became a much grimmer affair. It began to worry him. More and more the most important time of day became the evenings when he could get home and try once more to escape the ghosts. By then it wasn't just that he wanted to play the game. He simply had to play it.

Luck was against him. For some reason he fell ill. He started a cough. Every morning, when he got up, he felt rotten. He had to drag himself through each day. The only thing that kept him going was the thought of the games he could play at night.

His being ill worried his mum. She took him to the doctor but the doctor couldn't find much wrong with him and advised a few days off school. His mum put him to bed. She told him to read and to keep quiet. She told him not to play the game any more. But how could he stop? He went on playing and hid the set under the bedclothes whenever he heard her coming.

It was his dad who arranged for him to spend a long week-end in the country with his gran. He said the fresh air and the change would soon put Robin right again. Robb didn't mind the idea. He didn't really mind where he was so long as he could play the ghost game.

It had become all important. It was very worrying. Two or three weeks earlier he had almost won a game. He had been in sight of escape. Now he was getting worse, much worse. He was playing as badly as he had been playing right at the start. He fretted and coughed all the time. So he made sure that he took the game with him although his mother had told him not to.

'Have you left that game of yours up in your bedroom?' she checked as they were getting into the car to leave.

'Yes, Mum,' he lied, knowing it was safely hidden in his suitcase in the boot.

As soon as his parents had said goodbye and left his gran's house, he went up to his room and took the game out.

'What's that?' asked his gran who had followed him up. He explained, showing her how you played.

'Humphf!' she snorted. 'When I was a girl, we had better things to do. Come downstairs. Your tea's ready.'

At one time he had always enjoyed being at his gran's house. This time it felt different. She didn't give him much chance to play the game. She took him out for a walk. Then she found him small jobs to do. That night she asked him to play a card game. Then they watched television. When he went to bed, he felt too tired to play his ghost game.

The next day he felt worried and tense. In the morning his gran kept him busy as she usually did but in the afternoon he sneaked upstairs. He had played and lost several games before she came to look for him. She wanted him to go down to the village to carry some shopping. He knew it was no use arguing. On the way back, he thought of a plan.

That evening, he said he was tired and went to bed early. It gave him over an hour in which to play the game. As soon as he heard his gran getting ready to come up, he put his light out and pretended to be asleep. When she was safely in bed, he put the light on again and went on playing.

It wasn't fun. It was desperate. He kept making mistake after mistake. He struggled to get hold of himself, smothering his coughing so that his gran would not hear. But the ghosts were beginning to get him more and more easily. Each time he lost he could almost feel the touch of their thin, green tentacles and the pain as the metal voice spoke and his heart stopped.

It was much worse when he found himself inside the game. He was sitting in a small plastic dome in a long, pale-walled tunnel. It was half dark and he knew what was going to happen without the gloating metal voice.

'These are the cellars of the haunted house,' it told him. He could make out the words quite clearly. 'You will not get away. There is no escape.'

He was shivering and his hands were shaking but he managed to move the lever and the dome he was in moved gently forward. Then, soundlessly, from around the next corner, came a ghost. Its pale eyes glinted in its furry head and its green fangs gleamed savagely. He jerked the other lever.

In front of him a cross shone in the half-dark and the ghost slid away out of sight. Almost immediately the protecting light and the cross itself vanished. He pulled hard on the driving lever.

The dome lurched forward far too quickly. Another ghost appeared and he was almost on top of it, touching it, before he could stop and drive it away with another bright cross that flared and went out at once. He backed away and turned his head to see another ghost closing in from behind.

He stopped that one with a cross, moved the dome and found himself in a place where four dim, long tunnels crossed.

Ghosts were prowling towards him from all four directions. He fended them off with the crosses, his hand trembling almost too much to work the lever. Four more took their places. He sent out four more crosses. Other ghosts kept coming. He had no more crosses to use. His hands froze on the levers and he yelled in terror.

Suddenly, his gran was standing at the side of the dome. She opened the door and got in.

'Go, Robin!' she order. 'Move!' He was too scared to do anything. She took the levers from him and the dome jumped forward. A cross flashed in the air and the ghost ahead got out of the way. They were shaking and rattling along. He could see the door of escape at the end of the tunnel in front of them.

Then another green horror barred the way. Robin yelled again just as she sent another ghost-stopping cross towards it.

He opened his terrified eyes to find himself in his bedroom. His gran in her blue, woolly dressing-gown was shaking his shoulder.

'For Heaven's sake, wake up, Robin!' she ordered. 'You've been having a nightmare and I know why.'

'Ghosts,' he mumbled, hardly knowing where he was.

'Yes,' she said.'That's what you kept shouting.'

The game lay on the bed in front of him. She picked it up.

'It's this, isn't it?' she asked. He nodded,

without speaking.

'Daft!' she snorted. She moved towards the door, taking the game with her. 'Don't play it again, will you?'

'No, Gran.' He shook his head. 'I promise.'

And he never did.

Looking at the story again

1 What did the ghosts on the screen look like?

2 What did a 'ghost stopper' look like on the screen?

3 What sort of noise did the computer make if you reached the door of the haunted house?

4 How often had Robb heard that noise?

5 Where did he play the game at home?

6 What happened to his school work?

7 How did he keep going through the day when he first fell ill?

8 Why did his dad think that going to stay with his gran would help him?

9 How did his gran stop him playing the game at first?

10 What did he do one evening so that he could play the game?

11 How was the game different that evening?

12 What did the ghosts look like then?

13 Who saved him from the ghosts in the haunted house?

14 What did he do about the game after that?

Words

1 Find a word in the first paragraph meaning 'passages in a house or building' — it begins with

'c'. Find a word in the second paragraph meaning 'mysterious or ghostly' — it begins with 'e'. Find a word in the fourth paragraph meaning 'having ghosts in it' — it begins with 'h'. Use the three words in three sentences of your own.

2 'He started to cough.' All these words end in 'ough'. Write them out. The first letter of each word is given:

'Not smooth' — r_____

'Not tender' — t_____

'Part of a tree' — b_____

'Used to make bread' — d_____

Can you write down two more words that end 'ough'?

3 Write another name for the game played by Robb in the story.

4 '... because he lost all his games very quickly.' Complete these sentences with words of your own:

Because it was raining ...

... because the fire was out.

Because she was in a hurry ...

Writing

1 List any computer games you know *or* list some of the table games you can play at home.

2 Describe four or five sounds which you think are rather frightening.

3 A person goes into a shop to buy something rather expensive. You will have to decide what it is. In play form write out the conversation between the salesperson and the person who has come in to buy.

4 You take shelter in an old empty house. Then you find it is haunted. Are you alone? What do the ghosts look like? Do you get out safely?

The Old Sewing-Machine

Lisa clutched the ten pound note. She had been given it by her mother to buy material for a new tutu. She had been going to ballet school for four years. Her mother — they were a one-parent family — could not really afford it but Gran helped out from time to time. She really loved the ballet school although she was not as good as the other girls.

Now there was to be the annual competition at the school. Her tutu was ripped and too small so she could not enter unless she had a new one. She had plucked up courage to ask her mother; she knew she could not afford to buy one from the school and that her mother, who was not a good sempstress, would have to try making one.

Her mother had wearily agreed and now here she was clutching the ten pound note she suspected had come from Gran. The first shop she tried wanted fifteen pounds for the net material. What would she do if they were all like that? She could not possibly get more money.

Lisa tried three shops in the High Street. The prices ranged from fifteen to eighteen. In despair she had wandered down a narrow side street. Next to a hairdresser's there was a shop with a rather dirty window with the notice 'Remnants' in faded yellow paint. Two red fly-covered notices said 'SALE'.

She went in. A bell clanged as she did so. The shop was gloomy but the counter was heaped with remnants like a jumble sale. She might just find something here. An old, bent lady shuffled in from the back of the shop through a curtain. 'What is it, my dear?' she enquired. As she did so half-glasses slid down her nose.

Lisa explained.

'I expect we can find something here,' said the old lady.

'Will it be more than ten pounds?' asked Lisa.

'Let me see in your hand,' said the old lady.

'My hand?' queried Lisa. 'It is a ten pound note.'

'No, I want to see in your hand to read it.'

She picked up Lisa's hot hand with her own wizened brown-flecked one. 'Ah!' she sighed. 'The sign of the pirouette. You are the one who shall come.'

Lisa looked at her.

'Yes, you are the one.' With that she pulled out a splendid piece of stiff net from under the pile. 'This is what you want.' With some difficulty she wrapped it in old brown paper. She then turned and beckoned with her thin fingers. 'Come with me.'

Lisa wondered whether she dare. She had heard tales about young girls who had been lured into the backs of shops never to be seen again. But the old lady had such a smile on her face. It beamed out with pleasure. Lisa felt she couldn't disappoint her and she followed through the heavy curtain.

Half expecting some kind of Aladdin's cave, Lisa was disappointed by the room she found herself in. It was filled with cardboard boxes from floor to ceiling. But there were some gaps for faded pictures of a ballerina. The old lady was pointing to an old sewing-machine on the top of a shelf. 'Get that down, dear.'

With some difficulty, she was only ten, she struggled to take down the sewing-machine without it falling on her. It was black with gold lettering and there were lovely designs etched into the silver plates on the side. On one of the etchings was a ballerina on her toes.

'Now,' said the old lady. 'This is yours. You must promise me to make up the material for your tutu with this machine. It will then work happily for you for many years. Then when the time comes and you see the sign of the pirouette, you will know to whom to pass it on.'

With that she showed her out into the street. The bell clanged behind her and the old woman was gone. The machine was extremely heavy; she wondered how she would get it home. It would be difficult even to carry to the bus-stop. Then she remembered the ten pound note. She struggled to the High Street and managed to hail a taxi.

Her mother saw her getting out. She was furious that she had wasted her money so. When she saw the old sewing-machine she said it was only fit for the junk man who collected scrap iron. But she calmed down when she saw the material. Though on no account would they make up such good material on an old machine like that.

Lisa took the machine up to her bedroom. Immediately her fingers itched to sew something with it. She found a pattern for a tutu for a doll. She cut some strips from her old tutu and began.

The sewing-machine was worked by a handle on a wheel. From the moment she began she felt happy. It had a slight clattery purring noise. But the great joy was how the material glided through; it seemed to sew itself.

She took the doll's tutu down to her mother. 'That's beautiful!' she exclaimed. 'I didn't know you had the skill!'

'It's so easy on this machine, Mum,' she said excitedly. 'Can I please make my tutu on it?'

'I don't see why not with my help,' said her mother.

But her mother's help was not needed. She went away and left her to it. Lisa felt so much in harmony with the old sewing-machine as it clattered and purred making such fine stitching. Soon it was done. She put it on and paraded before her mother. 'You look lovely, darling,' she sighed. A tear twinkled in her eye.

At the dancing school all the girls and the few boys were chattering with excitement. This was the big day of the year. All the parents were there. There were cups and certificates to be won. Lisa changed into her new tutu. The other girls looked at her with envy; it was better than their bought ones. It was pure white yet it had a mysterious pink glow to it.

It came near her time to dance. She stood in the wings of the stage stretching her legs and pointing her toes. Her name was called. The notes struck up from the piano. An image of the old lady in the shop flashed through her mind. Then she was on.

From the moment she stepped on the stage she

felt a completely different dancer. Where before she had been stiff and mechanical she now glided and flowed. She had this great sense of lightness, of defying gravity. She could point, pirouette, leap and obtain her positions with ease. Her body felt like silver liquid in the tutu. She won great applause.

The dancing-teacher was amazed when she presented her with the cup as the best ten-year-old. She also received the cup as the most improved pupil.

Her mother put her arm around her in the bus going home. 'Whatever happens you must not give this up,' she said. 'We'll find the money somehow.'

Linda tried to explain about the sewing-machine and the tutu but it was not easy to put into words. 'You must go and thank the old lady then,' said her mother.

Next day she traced her route back to the side street and the old shop. But when she reached there it was newly boarded up and a sign said: 'CLOSED'. 'You looking for somebody?' asked a passing barrow-boy.

'The old lady who ran the shop,' Lisa told him.

'She passed away, dear, last night. Sad. She's been in that shop at least thirty years.'

Then Lisa knew why the image of the old lady had come into her mind just as she was about to step on stage. A few tears dropped down her cheek. She understood the sign of the pirouette.

Lisa became a great dancer. You would not recognize the name Lisa Smart because she changed it to a Russian name. She travelled the world dancing in the great theatres. But wherever she went she took the old sewing-machine with her. She knows one day she will need to pass it on to another young girl. She will see the sign in her hand. Who will it be?

Looking at the story again

1 What was the ten pounds for?
2 Who helped the family from time to time?
3 Why did Lisa not buy a tutu from the ballet school?
4 What was the word in the shop window that caught her eye?
5 What happened when she opened the shop door?
6 What strange thing does the old lady say to her?
7 How is the sewing-machine described?
8 How does she get home with the heavy machine?
9 What is surprising about the machine?
10 How well did Lisa dance in her new tutu?
11 How many cups did she win?
12 What happened to the old lady?
13 What does: 'She understood the sign of the pirouette' mean?
14 Why wouldn't you recognize the name 'Lisa Smart'?

Words

1 Describe in one sentence how you hold on to money you do not want to lose.
2 'courage' — write down four words ending in

'age' that have more than two letters before the 'age'.

3   The jobs of five people are mentioned in this story. Write them down and add five other jobs people do.

4   Write down the names of five different materials used for clothes.

5   'shuffled' — in one sentence describe an old person walking.

6   Give two meanings for these words: hail, tear, stage.

Writing

1   Write about something you found in a shop which changed your life. It could be a mysterious box or a book.

2   Write a poem called 'Machine Noises'. It need not rhyme.

3   Describe a shop you like to go in. Write at least six sentences.

4   What other kinds of show besides ballet might you see in a theatre? Make a list.

5   Write as a play the scene between Lisa, when she is old, and the young girl she hands the sewing-machine to.

Jason and the Grongans

The Grongans, who looked like large rocks, were arguing with raised voices. They were creatures who lived on the planet Vrakos. A small scout ship had just landed and it was the first time that a ship of that kind had ever visited Vrakos. The Grongans could not make up their minds what to do.

They were not arguing in human voices, of course. They were making loud crunching noises. Translated into English, it sounded something like this.

'Evil!' wailed Runk, the oldest Grongan. 'These are space demons. Devils! Grongan legend tells us so.'

'They are from a planet called Earth,' Brug, the scientist reported, using his view screen and information stored in the Grongan computer.

'Kill them! Destroy!' bellowed Krang, who was a warrior Grongan of high rank.

'Shouldn't we try to find out what they want first?' Nork, a lady Grongan, asked.

'No!' roared Krang. 'Kill!'

'How do we know we can?' asked Brug, consulting the screen and the computer. 'They're armed. If we attack them, they might kill us first.'

Silence fell. The Grongans thought about this. Then the argument went on but more quietly.

In the end it was decided not to attack the ship.

The Grongans would send out a small party, led by the great Krang, to spy first on the Earth people.

Captain Boyd and the two scientists were about to leave the scout ship and explore. There was air on Vrakos and the planet had almost Earth gravity so they did not have to wear space suits. They left Jason, Captain Boyd's son, and Jason's friend, Chris, behind. Captain Boyd had taken Jason along on the trip to keep him out of harm's way. People at Home Base complained too often about the mischief Jason got up to. Many of them spoke of him as a 'holy terror'.

Jason, himself, had complained so much about being taken along as a kind of prisoner that, in the end, his father had allowed Chris to come along as company.

Captain Boyd looked at his son sternly. 'You are on no account to leave this ship,' he commanded. 'Understand?'

'Yes, Dad.' Jason looked at him innocently.

'If you do, you young monkey,' warned his father. 'I'll wring your neck.'

'Oh, no, Dad,' said Jason, as if he meant every word of it.

His father glared at him distrustfully. Then he snorted and left the ship with the two scientists. From the view port, Jason watched until the three were out of sight. Then he turned to Chris.

'Come on,' he said.

'Where?' asked Chris, surprised.

'Down the ladder and out. We'll have a look at this place.'

'But your Dad!' Chris protested.

'He'll never know,' said Jason. 'We'll be back

long before he is.'

'I don't know.' Chris shook his head. He had been in trouble with Jason before.

'We won't do any harm,' Jason argued. 'We'll just have a look round and a bit of a muck about.'

'You said you wouldn't.'

'I had my fingers crossed when I said it. Come on!' Jason picked up his bag and led the way down the ladder.

Before they had walked very far, he stopped, rummaged in his bag and pulled something out.

'What's that?' asked Chris, much interested.

'A catapult.'

'Where did you get it?'

'I made it. There was a picture and a description in a very old book back at Home Base. I worked things out, got hold of some rubber and a piece of forked metal and here it is.'

'What does it do?'

'I'll show you,' said Jason. He took a small pebble out of his bag and fitted it into the catapult. A lump of rock was sticking out above a rise in the ground not far away. Jason aimed and fired. The pebble hit the dome of rock with a loud 'Spang!' and burst into a hundred pieces. The lump of rock disappeared.

'Terrific!' said Chris. 'Let me try.'

They took turns in using the catapult until all Jason's pebbles had gone.

The lump of rock had been Krang's head. Ferg and Werg, his trusty helpers, had carried him back to Grongan headquarters. Now, conscious again, and wearing a cement bandage, he was ready to report.

'I sighted two mighty Earth warriors and crept closer,' he said.

'They were two children,' Brug, the scientist, said coldly. He had been watching what happened on his view screen and reading the computer.

'I was immediately under fire,' Krang went on, scowling. 'I was hit by a powerful weapon. Probably atomic. Very modern. Unknown to me.'

'It was a catapult,' Brug told him sighing. 'A very old and very primitive Earth weapon.'

'Oh!' grunted Krang. He fell silent.

'Doom!' wailed Runk. 'Doom has come to Vrakos.'

'Do shut up, Runk,' Nork snapped. 'We've got to *think*.'

After more noisy discussion, they decided to use the Death-Scent Machine, feared by all Grongans. The view screen showed two parties of Earth people. There were three big ones a good way from Grongan headquarters and there were two smaller figures much nearer. The plan was to use the Machine on the two little figures. They were an easier target.

Ferg and Werg were not eager to put the Machine in place but, as soldiers, they had to obey orders. They carried the Machine out, careful not to be seen. They placed it on the path that the small Earth people would take, switched it on and trundled back to headquarters to watch what happened.

Jason stopped suddenly. 'Pooh!' he said and sniggered.

'Yes,' Chris sniffed. 'Like rotten eggs.' He giggled. 'Where's it coming from?'

'Here.' Jason pointed to a strange object made of bits of metal and stone. He reeled back. 'Cor! Mouldy cheese!' he snorted.

'Rotten fish!' Chris, too, found it a huge joke.

'Sweaty feet!' Jason gurgled.

They tottered about, almost helpless with laughter as they thought of even more disgusting things to suggest to each other.

'There!' Krang pointed excitedly to the two small figures on the viewing screen. 'See? The Death-Scent is working. They're staggering. They'll fall down soon.'

'They're laughing,' Brug told him glumly, looking at the computer. 'They must think the Death-Scent is funny.'

'Funny!' choked Krank and fell silent.

Runk started to wail so much that he had to be sent out. Further plans simply had to be made.

Nork suggested that they should use the Grongan Capture Net. The two small Earth people could then be brought in and investigated.

Ferg and Werg, who would have to carry and use the net, said at once that they thought this was a very silly idea. Krang, however, liked it. He reminded Ferg and Werg that they were soldiers and that the penalty for mutiny was being ground to a fine powder. So they got the net and left.

Jason and Chris were having a sit down in the shade. Ferg and Werg crept closer with the Capture Net.

'Bit of music?' Jason asked.

'Good idea,' Chris agreed.

Jason got out his cassette Mega-Player and switched on a tape of the new group, the 'Asteroid

Blasters'. They were thrashing away at maximum power with their new hit 'Super-Nova'. Jason turned the volume up full. He leaned back against the bank and Chris leaned back with him. Neither said anything. They didn't want to talk. They couldn't have done, even if they had wanted to. It was impossible to hear anyone speak. The music was deafening.

Ferg and Werg were back at Grongan headquarters. The net trailed limply behind them.

'Well?' Krang demanded.

'We couldn't get near them,' Ferg whined. Little shocks, like tiny earthquakes, were still running through his body.

'They had a Soundwave Machine.' Werg seemed on the brink of tears. 'It pierced me to the core.'

'It was so loud,' Ferg agreed. 'It was awful. Awful!'

'Fools!' Krang snarled.

The other Grongans looked at each other desperately.

'We'll just have to go and make peace with these Earth people,' Nork said.

'Never!' bellowed Krang and winced. Bellowing made his head ache. 'Surrender?' he went on more quietly. 'Grongans never surrender. I, the great Krang, will face them again. I shall defeat them with the Hero Fall.'

The rest looked at each other doubtfully.

The Grongan Hero Fall was an ancient form of attack which had fallen out of favour recently. You stood by the path your enemy would take, keeping very still and pretending to be an ordinary rock. When he passed, you fell on him. The Hero Fall, though, did not always work. Your enemy might dodge at the last moment. Then, if you fell heavily, it could knock all the wind out of you and you would be at the enemy's mercy.

No one reminded Krang of this, however. He was obviously in no mood to be argued with. They watched him go.

'What are you doing?' Chris asked. Ahead of him, Jason had stepped aside from the path. He was fumbling in his bag.

'This'll puzzle the next lot to visit this place,' he said. He was standing on one side of a large, gnarled stone. His hand came out of the bag with a red paint spray. On the stone he wrote. 'JB was here. Asteroid Blasters rule OK'

He stepped back in surprise as the stone toppled slowly forward and fell across the path.

'That could have been dangerous,' Chris told him.

'I suppose it could,' said Jason. He aimed the spray and put a big red full stop after the letters 'OK' on the stone.

'Hadn't we better be getting back?' Chris urged nervously. 'We don't want your Dad to catch us out of the ship.'

'He won't,' Jason calmed him. 'Bags of time.'

'I'm going, anyway.'

'All right. All right. No rush.'

Chris hurried off. Jason followed more slowly, whistling and frowning slightly. He was thinking it funny that they had seen no real signs of life all the time they had been out.

The large stone had, of course, been Krang. The paint spray had filled up many of his breathing holes and he had fainted for lack of air. Ferg and Werg who had been watching him from a safe distance had come up and brought him round as soon as the boys had gone.

Now, almost recovered, but coughing from time to time, he was back in the Grongan headquarters. He looked rather broken and defeated. He was still slightly paint-stained too.

'Peace,' he whispered hoarsely. 'We must go and make peace with these invaders.'

'I told you we'd have to,' Nork said. He glared at her.

When the exploration party returned to the ship, the first thing that Captain Boyd did was to check up on Jason. Jason, though, was where he had been left. Captain Boyd could hardly believe it. He looked suspiciously round the cabin. Everything looked to be in order.

'What have you been up to?' he demanded.

'Nothing, Dad.' Jason gazed back innocently. He knew he was in the clear. Chris wouldn't give anything away. There was no chance that his father would ever find out how they had spent the afternoon.

'Chris?' asked Captain Boyd. Chris shook his head, evidently fascinated by the book he was reading.

Captain Boyd would dearly have liked to investigate further but one of the scientists hurried in. A party of strange rock-like creatures were gathering outside the ship. They seemed to want something. Captain Boyd was needed at once to operate the Galactic Translating Machine.

Captain Boyd followed the scientist out, thinking. Jason's behaviour was too good to be true. Further enquiries would have to be made. He was sure Jason had been up to something that afternoon. But what exactly?

He didn't know that, after the peace treaty had been signed, Krang and Nork and Brug and the other Grongans would be the ones to tell him.

Looking at the Story Again

1 What did the Grongans look like?

2 What did Krang want to do at first to the visitors from Earth?

3 Why had the people at Home Base asked Captain Boyd to take his son, Jason, with him?

4 How did Chris feel about Jason's idea that they should leave the ship?

5 How had Jason managed to make the catapult?

6 What did Jason think he was firing the catapult at?

7 What sort of weapon did Krang say that Jason had used?

8 What did the Grongans decide to use next against the Earth people?

9 Why do you think that Ferg and Werg said that using the Capture Net was a silly idea?

10 What stopped Ferg and Werg from using the Capture Net?

11 How did you use the Grongan Hero Fall against an enemy?

12 What made Krang faint and fall over?

13 What tells you that Captain Boyd had not

trusted Jason to keep out of mischief?

14 How was he going to learn what Jason had been doing all day?

Words

1 In the first section of the story, find the words that mean 'spoke in a high, sad voice as if he was crying' and 'shouted very loudly' and write them down.

2 Write this out, punctuating it properly:

come on he said where asked chris surprised down the ladder and out well have a look at this place but your dad chris protested

Now check with the story to see that you have got it right.

3 What do you do if you 'rummage' in something?

4 What other word in the story means almost the same as 'distrustfully'? (It describes the way Captain Boyd looks round the cabin when he comes back.)

5 When Ferg and Werg do not want to carry the Capture Net, Krang reminds them of something. What two words used there mean 'punishment' and 'rebellion by soldiers against officers'?

Writing

1 List five pop songs you like most at the moment and then list your three favourite pop groups or pop stars.

2 Write your own story about some people who make the first landing on a strange planet.

The Spell

'Look!' Joan held it out on the palm of her hand. 'Isn't it — strange?'

'Yes,' Katie, her younger sister, agreed doubtfully. The stone was black. Had someone carved it or had the sea rounded it into that shape? It looked like a figure with arms, legs and a head. Still wet from the sea, it glittered and winked on Joan's open hand.

'Throw it away,' Katie said.

'Don't be silly.' Joan stared at her, surprised. 'I'm going to keep it.' She wrapped it carefully in her handkerchief and put it away in her pocket. Then she walked on with a narrow, secret smile on her lips.

Katie followed, frowning. Something seemed to have gone wrong with the day.

They had come down without their parents to stay for a fortnight at Dalsey Bay with Aunty Madge who kept a guest-house. Joan, always cheerful and friendly and helpful, was a great success with the people staying there right from the start. Even Katie, who was quieter and more shy, felt at home very quickly.

Every day they had had bright, sunny weather. They helped Aunty Madge in the guest-house but they had plenty of time for themselves and there were plenty of things to do. There was a cliff top near the house from which you could see for miles.

Then there were the cobbled streets of red-roofed houses to explore and there was always the beach, pebbled but with stretches of sand. Joan, as usual, had made a lot of new friends for them both.

On the way back to the guest-house that morning, though, Joan seemed to be in a peculiar, dark and silent mood. It was most unlike her; it lasted all day. That evening Katie could stand it no longer.

'What's the matter with you?' she asked.

'Me?' said Joan.

'You're — funny.'

'Am I?' Joan smiled. 'Why don't you laugh then?'

'I didn't mean that.' Katie turned away. She didn't feel like laughing.

Next day things started badly and got worse. Breakfast went wrong for the guests. Aunty Madge couldn't think why. Joan seemed strangely pleased by all the upset. That worried Katie. Joan didn't want to go out nor did she make any offer to help with the work. It was Katie who went down to the shops for Aunty Madge. What she saw when she came back worried her even more. As soon as she had given the shopping to Aunty Madge, she looked for Joan. Joan was back upstairs in their room.

'Why was Darren crying just now?' Katie challenged. Darren was a small boy staying in the guest-house.

'I don't know.' Joan shrugged. She looked lovingly at what she held in her hand.

'You were with him. Were you teasing him?'

'Why would I do that?' Joan asked carelessly.

'It certainly looked like it.'

'Did it really?' Joan smiled mockingly.

Katie could think of nothing to say. Suddenly it was like talking to a complete stranger. Normally Joan liked children and they certainly liked her. Now she seemed as cold and as hard as the queerly-shaped black stone she was holding.

Katie went downstairs and out of the house. Wherever she walked a fear that was slightly crazy haunted her and at last her feet took her to the beach. She was glad to see Mr and Mrs Pearson, two old people who had lived in Dalsey Bay all their lives. They had first made friends with Joan and Katie one breezy day on the beach. The wind had taken Mrs Pearson's newspaper and then Mr Pearson's hat and the two girls had dashed about gathering the things up.

The Pearsons asked where Joan was, talked about the splendid weather and then Mr Pearson began, as usual, to talk about old times in Dalsey. He told Katie again about the fishing fleet there had been and the things that fishermen used to believe would bring them good luck.

'And bad luck, too,' he said. 'Did I tell you about the witches?'

'Oh, George!' said Mrs Pearson.

'Witches?' Katie asked.

'There were supposed to be a lot of them here last century,' he went on. 'You had to be careful then. A lot of people were scared of their magic and the things they could do. They would use all sorts of strange things — little dolls, bits of knotted string, carved things in wood and stone — to carry their evil spells.'

'Evil spells!' scoffed Mrs Pearson. 'That's all

just silly talk. You'll frighten the child.'

'I'm not frightened,' said Katie, though she was.

'I'm only telling her what people used to say,' Mr Pearson protested. He looked at the cheerful holiday crowd on the sunlit beach. 'It seems daft now, though, to think that anyone could believe in such things.'

As soon as she could, Katie said she had to get back to the guest-house because she had a job to do. When she got home, she went straight up to Joan.

'Give it to me,' she ordered.

'What?' Joan teased her.

'That black stone.'

'What for?' Joan held it out to her.

'I'm going to get rid of it.'

As soon as she moved to take it, Joan clenched her hand on it and laughed. Anger and fear choked Katie. She grabbed Joan's fist and tried to wrench the stone away. But Joan was much too strong. She twisted Katie's wrist until Katie fell to her knees and the pain brought tears to her eyes. Katie struggled free at last and left the room, her throat tight and thick with emotion.

Should she tell Aunty Madge? Would Aunty Madge believe her or would she simply think that Katie was being over-imaginative and silly? Was she, in fact, imagining things? She felt so confused that she didn't know what to do. Her head was swimming. And soon she found it hard to tell anyone anything. It was not just emotion that had choked her. Her throat really was sore. Before long when she tried to speak her voice cracked and croaked. Aunty Madge took her temperature, looked troubled and put her to bed at once.

There, mercifully, Katie slept. Aunty Madge woke her after a couple of hours with something to eat on a tray. Katie, however, could not touch it. She even found it hard to swallow the drink Aunty Madge had brought her.

'I've rung the doctor,' Aunty Madge said. 'He can't get here until first thing tomorrow. I hope you're going to be all right.'

Katie nodded feebly and then drifted off into that uneasy sleep that felt like drowning.

When she awoke next time, Joan was looking down at her. The curtains were drawn but there was enough light to see the little black stone figure she was holding out.

'You know why you're ill, don't you?' Joan taunted. 'It's him. He's having his revenge. You wanted to get rid of him but he's stopped all that, hasn't he?'

Katie tried to speak but could only croak.

'Oh, yes,' Joan went on. 'He's a very lively little imp. I'll bet you can't guess what he's going to do tomorrow.' For a moment she stood there smiling so that in the dim light her eyes and teeth gleamed. She didn't look like Joan at all. Then she moved away to switch on the light and get ready for bed. Half-asleep and half-awake, Katie watched in a kind of dreamy terror. At last Joan got into the other bed, slid the stone under the pillow and lay down, turning her back and turning off the light.

Sleep sucked Katie down into a world of dark and horrid dreams. One woke her at last. She dreamed she was in her bed in the bedroom. A

84

weight was on her chest, a black figure. It had pointed ears and it winked its slanting eyes at her.

'Alone,' it whispered. 'You're all alone, aren't you? No help, anywhere.'

She sat up, wide awake with her heart pounding. Her head was spinning, too, but she found strength from somewhere.

When she got out of bed she shook all over but she forced herself to make no noise at all. Slowly, and holding herself stock-still each time Joan moved in her sleep, she felt under the pillow. When her fingertips touched the cold stone it seemed to try to slither away but in the end she had it in her grasp. Then, picking up shoes, jeans and a pullover she slipped downstairs and dressed in the hall.

Then she had to sit down. Her throat felt raw; if she swallowed it was like swallowing knives. Her head thudded and stabbed with sudden blinding pain. But she opened the front door and went like a shadow into the street.

Outside, the stone felt like a block of ice in her pocket and its cold crept through her body. The street lamps were dim and her feet dragged so slowly that she wondered if she had ever left her bed at all. Was she still moving through another vague, frightening dream? A wind in her face pushed and tugged at her making her stagger.

She could hardly think. Where was she going? She wandered aimlessly. Once she found herself nearly back at the guest-house. She stopped and tried to clear her mind. The sea — that was it! The stone had to go back to the sea. Under the cliff the water was deep. Down there the stone could do no harm.

It was easier after that. The wind had changed and was at her back, almost forcing her along. She went fast up the last stretch of cliff path and faster across the grass on the cliff top that led to the edge.

Realisation came nearly too late. She was not taking the stone to the sea. It was taking her. It could not stop her from putting an end to its evil magic but it could destroy her with it.

Terror gave her strength. She took the thing, now as heavy as lead, from her pocket and flung it out into space to fall into the waves on the rocks below. Then she was able to fall gasping and sobbing on her face only a step from the sheer drop.

She sat up. The wind had dropped. Her head no longer hurt; her mind was no longer confused. The rawness had gone from her throat but she felt empty and very tired. She got back into the house quietly enough, though, and, taking off only her shoes, fell into bed and was immediately asleep.

She woke up to find Joan, fully dressed, watching her.

'It's gone, hasn't it?' Joan asked.

'Yes,' Katie nodded.

'Phew! What a relief.' Joan paused. 'It was like being mad, you know.'

'I know.'

Joan grinned at her, her old broad cheerful grin. 'Thanks,' she said. She came across and hugged Katie. 'Thanks. You don't know how much.' She went to the door. 'I feel like breakfast. You'd better stay there until the doctor's been. I'll bring you some up.' She went out. Katie could hear her singing on the way downstairs.

Katie jumped out of bed and went to the window. It was another brilliant day. She might have to argue with Aunty Madge about it but she certainly wasn't going to stay in bed. They could tell the doctor not to come. She felt like singing, too — and running and jumping and shouting for joy. The last thing she wanted was bed and a doctor on a perfect day like this.

Looking at the story again

1 What did the black stone look like?

2 Who were Joan and Katie staying with?

3 In what way did Joan change after she found the stone?

4 Which two old people did Katie meet when she went for a walk?

5 What did the witches of Dalsey Bay use in former times to carry their magic spells?

6 Why could Katie not take the black stone away from Joan?

7 What happened to Katie after she had tried to take the stone away from Joan?

8 What, according to Joan, had caused Katie's illness?

9 After she had dreamed about the stone, what did Katie do?

10 When she had it in her pocket, how did the stone feel and what did it do?

11 How did she feel when she had thrown the stone over the cliff?

12 What sort of mood was Joan in when Katie told her she had got rid of the stone?

Words

1 'the palm of her hand' — what other kind of 'palm' is there?

2 What kind of animals 'slither'? What kind of animals 'croak'?

3 What might you see drifting on a river? What might drift across the sky on a calm day?

4 What is an 'imp'? Can you think of two other words which mean the same thing?

5 If you walk about a town 'aimlessly', what are you doing?

6 'What she saw worried her even more.' Complete these sentences with your own words:

What he hoped for ...

What she told me ...

What they bought from the shop ...

Writing

1 Describe some of the things you would like to find in a seaside town. It might be somewhere you have visited or it might be an imaginary place.

2 Write about either a very friendly person or a very unfriendly person. It could be someone you know or someone you imagine.

3 Write a poem called 'The Top of the Cliffs' or 'The High Wind' or 'The Bad Dream'.

4 Mr Pearson from the story or another old person talks about the times when he or she was young. Write down what you think he or she would say.

5 Write a story about a witch who tries to cast a magic spell on someone. What is the spell supposed to do? Harm the person or help?

The Voice in the Wind

Atifa and her friends played happily climbing the old chestnut tree. It had stood on the edge of the village green of Sumpton for seventy years now. It had been a 'house' for them as little children and then a 'jungle' to play Tarzan in. Today it was a 'strange planet'.

All the village children loved the tree. It was conker time. Some boys from another village came up and began to throw sticks. Atifa yelled at them but they did not stop. She and Alison and Robbie had to scramble down quickly.

One of the sticks clattered against Mr Donkin's fence. His cottage was next to the tree. He was a red-faced man with a big purple-veined nose who often worked a night shift and slept during the day. He hated children playing in the tree. He was known as 'Elephant' because he was often said to be drunk. This came from 'elephant's trunk' in the Cockney rhyming slang and had been given him by Robbie. 'Elephant' came running out now and chased the boys away with a stick. Then he turned to Atifa and her friends: 'Now you clear off as well!' he yelled.

'We're entitled to play here,' said Atifa. 'It's public property.'

'You're not entitled to make all that noise and to damage my property!'

'We didn't.'

'Clear off!' He came for them in a menacing way. They ran.

It was Friday. Atifa's father was reading the local paper. 'Oh,' he exclaimed, 'they're going to cut down the tree on the village green.'

'Not the conker tree!' exploded Atifa.

'It must be that one. The Parish Council says it's unsafe and could fall on a cottage. That would be Mr Donkin's. Oh, I see he's Chairman of the Parish Council.'

'It's a swindle,' shouted Atifa. 'We climb the tree all the time. He chases us off.'

'Well, it says a survey has been done and the tree's unsafe. Don't climb it anymore.'

Atifa ran to the village green. If there was one thing that she was going to do it was to climb that tree despite her father and silly old Elephant. She clambered up high into its branches. She stretched out and swung to her favourite spot between the fork of two branches. Here you could rest as on a bed. She lay looking up at the tracery of branches above. They swayed in the high wind like dancing ballerinas. They had a soothing hypnotic effect. She forgot to think if silly old Elephant was watching out of his window.

She thought she had been there five minutes when she heard the voice. It was not a human voice; it was a voice that drifted like a tune through her brain; a long musical note as though played on chime bars; a voice that seemed to come from the depths of the universe: 'Save me! Save me!'

She lay there lulled by the voice. It was not

frightening in any way, yet it was so real and unhuman. Finally it faded, like a long echo going down a tunnel, a tunnel of time.

Atifa scrambled to a sitting position. She looked up at the waving branches. Was it the wind? Had she fallen asleep and dreamed it all? Whatever the reason, she knew the tree must be saved. It had cried out for help!

Her father found out that the tree was to come down on the following Tuesday. Atifa went to her bedroom and wrote thirty notes to each member of her class. On the front it said: SECRET. Inside it said: Meet at the conker tree after school tonight. Atifa.

During the Monday the children clustered around Atifa in the playground, but she would only repeat what she had said in the note and that it was a great secret.

After school they all turned up round the base of the tree.

'What is the great secret?' asked Martin Jarvis in a sneering way.

Atifa told them about the tree having to come down. They were shocked. Then she told them about her experience. Only Martin Jarvis sneered at this but the rest shouted him down. What could they do? Atifa said, 'I have a plan. Now listen ...'

Atifa's parents were going mad next morning. Where was she? Her bed had been slept in but she was nowhere to be found. They rang Alison's house. More consternation! Alison was not there either! The police were informed. Other parents rang Atifa's family. Their children were missing.

Soon a message came back. The whole of Atifa's class were sitting in the conker tree. A banner at the top said: SAVE OUR TREE.

Atifa was in her favourite nook. She lay back and relaxed. As the wind rose the voice of the tree came to her again. 'Save me! Save me!'

'The tree is talking to me!' she cried out. 'Listen!'

The children listened. The wind rustled through the leaves.

'I can hear it,' exclaimed Robbie. 'It's like the tinkling of glass.'

'That's it,' said Atifa.

'So can I!' shouted Alison. 'It's speaking to me.'

One by one the children took up the cry. 'The tree is talking to us.'

Even Martin Jarvis cried out.

The children were oblivious to the fact that below them were a police car, an ambulance and a fire truck. A policeman was climbing up.

'Look, love, are you coming down?' he urged Alison.

She looked through him as though he wasn't there.

He tried Atifa. She saw no policeman. She heard only the tree.

The policeman tried to speak to some of the others. Then he climbed down. 'They're in some kind of trance up there. They look through you and don't speak. It would be dangerous to try and force them down.'

Atifa's father climbed the tree. 'Don't be so silly, Atifa. Come down at once.' The glazed look in her eyes told him she did not see him. He climbed down.

By now most of the village had gathered round the tree. The men who were going to cut it down had arrived as well. 'Elephant' was stamping about. 'Silly young fools!' he yelled. 'This tree is coming down despite their silly tricks!'

'If we wait they will come down,' said a police inspector. 'They'll get hungry.'

They waited. But the children did not come down. They did not even stir. The parents were getting very anxious. At tea-time they were still there. Then it began to get dark. Some of the mothers were crying now. 'They'll fall out in the dark,' they cried. 'Do something!'

'I think the only thing to get them down is a promise not to cut the tree down.'

'Never!' cried Mr Donkin. 'I'll not be beaten by a bunch of kids!'

But the other parents overruled him.

The police inspector took up a loud hailer. 'We'll do all we can to save the tree,' he yelled.

Nothing happened at first. Then slowly the children began to stir.

'Are they coming down?' said Atifa's mother anxiously.

'Is that a real promise?' cried Atifa. It was the first word any child had spoken for eleven hours.

'It's a real promise,' said Atifa's father.

'We'll come down then.'

Slowly the children appeared at the bottom of the tree. They were hugged by grateful parents and taken home and fed. Next day a new survey of the tree was made. It was not as bad as the Parish Council had said. It could be saved.

The children were jubilant. Mr Donkin said that

if a gang of kids was going to run the village, he was leaving. After school Atifa climbed the tree alone. She lay snugly in her nook. There was not a breath of wind but she distinctly heard the words: 'Thank you. Thank you, Atifa.'

Looking at the story again

1 What kind of tree did the children play in?
2 Mention two games they played in it.
3 Who lives near the tree?
4 Why does he not like the children playing there?
5 What does the first survey say about the tree?
6 What words does Atifa think she hears coming from the tree?
7 What did Atifa's note say?
8 Who goes to sit in the tree on the Tuesday morning?
9 What does the banner say?
10 How many children hear the voice?
11 Why do the police not force them down?
12 What does the police inspector decide to do instead? Does it work?
13 Why do the parents decide to do all they can to save the tree?
14 What other words does Atifa hear?

Words

1 Write down five different kinds of tree. Spell them with small letters.
2 What words are used to describe Mr Donkin?

Can you think of any other words that might suit him?

3 Finish these expressions in your own words:
The branches swayed like ...
the leaves danced like ...
the voice of the tree sounded like ...

4 What words rhyme with 'tree'? How many can you think of?

5 Do you know any cockney rhyming slang? What do these mean: apples and pears; tit for tat; pig's ear?

Writing

1 What are the rules for a game of conkers in your school? Write them down.

2 Imagine you climbed a high tree. Describe how you climbed up. Describe what you can see from the top.

3 Try a rhymed poem about a tree. You might use some of the words you listed.

4 In about three sentences describe what it is like to saw wood.

5 As a play, write about the conversation the children have in the playground the day after the tree has been saved.